"A new and splendid edifice"

Anne Ross	The architecture of the University of Glasgow
John Hume	Photographs

University
of Glasgow
Press   1975

© University of Glasgow 1975

ISBN 0 85261 125 0

This guide to the buildings of the University of Glasgow has been published to coincide with an Exhibition of the same title featuring the University's architecture. The Exhibition is the University's contribution to European Architectural Heritage Year.

Anne Ross is the deputy archivist of the University of Glasgow.

John Hume lectures in History in the University of Strathclyde.

Printed by Robert MacLehose and Co. Ltd
Anniesland, Glasgow

ACKNOWLEDGEMENTS

Anne Ross, John Hume and Michael Moss, the University archivist, wish to thank the following people without whose help this publication and the accompanying Exhibition "A New and Splendid Edifice" would not have been possible: Professor L. Alcock, Professor A. A. M. Duncan, Professor A. MacMillan, Dr. Ian Rolfe, Roger Billcliffe, the Secretary of the University Court, the Planning and Buildings Office, David Walker and Robert Cowper. Thanks are also due to R. Burnett, the Glasgow School of Art, for printing and enlarging the photographs, and to Ron Harrison for designing the Exhibition.

Plates 1–3 are by T. & R. Annan.

PREFACE

European Architectural Heritage year is intended to bring to public attention the richness and diversity of the architectural heritage of the European peoples; to manifest the cultural importance of place and building in establishing and confirming national, community and personal identity; and above all to engender awareness of the fragility of the built environment under the pressure of economic change and self interest.

In welcoming our University contribution to Heritage year – publication of an account of the past and present buildings of the University – can it be hoped that the fine photographs and scholarly and informative text will not only arouse interest in and awareness of the historic associations and visual beauty which the physical surroundings of the University campus have to offer, but will encourage a positive appreciation of the life-enhancing contribution of architecture in the built environment, and an understanding of the traditional responsibility vested in the University in its institutional role as a client and patron of the Arts?

This is especially important in Glasgow where the continuing erosion of the city's fabric and the virtually inconceivable record of recent and planned loss of civic and architectural landmarks threaten to leave us devoid of any historic or cultural continuity and render meaningless the familiar boast, 'I belong to Glasgow'.

Anne Ross and John Hume are to be congratulated on their joint creative achievement in this booklet and the exhibition.

Andrew MacMillan
Professor of Architecture

The Old College

"One of the finest, and certainly (the) most extensive specimen of Scottish civil architecture of the seventeenth century" is the description accorded by MacGibbon & Ross to the Old College buildings on the eastern side of the High Street which were started in 1632 and survived until 1870.

After its foundation in 1451, the University, which consisted only of the Faculty of Arts, held classes in the Chapter House of the Cathedral and subsequently in a house in the Rottenrow. As early as 1470, it had established itself in the High Street with the aid of gifts of adjoining properties from James, first Lord Hamilton, and Sir Thomas of Arthurlie and a further endowment of land and money was received from Queen Mary in 1560. No adequate description of these buildings survives except that they were tenements with some open ground behind.

With the disruption of its ecclesiastical dependence by the Reformation, the University had fallen into decay. But the Nova Erectio – a Charter under the Great Seal of James VI, dated 1577, obtained by the efforts of Principal Andrew Melville – laid down a new constitution and provided revenues and thereafter the University began once more to flourish.

By the beginning of the seventeenth century, with the increasing number of students, the buildings were becoming inadequate and in 1632 new buildings were begun by Principal Sharp in the garden ground behind the High Street and continued under the succeeding Principal, Patrick Gillespie. By 1660 the original tenements had been pulled down and the new buildings were completed by a handsome façade and gateway (Pl. 1).

The College front extended along the High Street for about 285 feet with the main gateway in the centre. This gateway passed under the Fore or Faculty Hall, with the Janitor's or Porter's lodge on the north and the Registrar's office on the south. Within was a court of irregular shape, measuring 80 by 40 feet with buildings on all sides. In the south-western corner the Lion and Unicorn staircase led down from the Fore Hall and on the eastern side was the tower, built in 1656 from a donation by Zachary Boyd, Minister of the Barony and Rector of the University (Pl. 2). An

PLATE 1
The Old College from College Street. The façade was the culmination of the buildings begun in 1632.

arched passage passed beneath the tower into a somewhat larger inner court. The north and east sides of this court formed the earliest part of the building, the north wing bearing the date 1639 above one of the windows. McGibbon & Ross commented: "The work of the inner courtyard of the College, which is the earliest part of the structure, shows a good deal of the character of the simple Scottish style, while the later portions indicate the importance of Renaissance features from abroad, very similar in design to the work at Heriot's Hospital (Edinburgh). The entrance gateway and the front to the High Street, the outer gateway under the tower, the scroll ornaments over the window, the Doric arcade in the outer courtyard, the staircase to the 'fore buildings', the chimneys and other details all savour strongly of the style which prevailed in Germany and the Low Countries in the seventeenth century."

Although the 1632 buildings were built with growth in mind, the expansion far outpaced the contemplation of it. Extensions and improvements were carried out from time to time as the number of students and the fields of study increased. The Library, which was originally accommodated in the east side of the inner court, moved to a new building behind the main block which was completed in 1744 from plans by William Adam. The whole eastern side of the inner court was replaced by a fine new building in Grecian Doric style, with larger class rooms and a new common hall above. Designed by Peter Nicholson and completed in 1811, it was paid for in part by the bequest of Robert Hamilton, a merchant in Canton, and was known as the Hamilton Building.

Immediately to the north of the main building and extending the full depth was the Professors' court, with houses on the north and east sides and a house for the Professor of Anatomy on the south side of the gateway. The earliest of these houses was started in 1722 and others were built as funds permitted and the number of professors increased. The Principal's house, with its own court and garden, was to the south of the main buildings and faced the High Street.

A little to the south, at the back of the College was the College church, which had originally been the Convent of the Blackfriars. After the Reformation the order in Scotland was dissolved and the church and manse given to the University by Queen Mary in 1563. When the building of the 1632 College was in progress the town took over the church and main-

PLATE 2
The Tower of the Old College from the Inner Court. In a niche above the archway is a bust of Zachary Boyd.

tained it but it continued to be used for University worship until 1764 when chapel services began to be held in the Common Hall. The church, which had been struck by lightning and burned in 1670, rebuilt and opened for worship in 1702, was finally swept away with the other College buildings after 1870.

The Hunterian Museum, which occupied a site behind the College, was a handsome building in the style of the classical revival, erected in 1804 from designs by William Stark, a gifted architect of the day. It was built to house Dr. William Hunter's Collection which he had bequeathed to the University on his death in 1783, together with £8,000 for a building to contain it (Pl. 3).

With the increasing unattractiveness of the centre of a growing industrial city during the first half of the nineteenth century, the desire to move to the cleaner and more fashionable West-End became very strong. In 1845, when the University was approached by the Glasgow, Airdrie and Monklands Junction Railway Company who wished to acquire the College property for the terminus of a proposed railway to Airdrie in exchange for a new University to be built by them on the west of the city, the scheme was viewed with enthusiasm.

An Act of Parliament allowing the College to dispose of its buildings and grounds received the Royal Assent in 1846 and an Agreement was drawn up with the Railway Company. The Company purchased the lands of Woodlands and commissioned John Baird, a Glasgow architect, to draw up plans. Three different schemes were conceived by Baird over as many years, each accompanied by much controversy, disagreement and discussion. The first, "E" shaped, in the Scottish style, with classical features internally, was considered insufficient in size; the second (Pl. 4) with two quadrangles in a hybrid style with Italian and Scottish features, was considered to have inadequate light in the quadrangles; and the third, similar in style to the second but with one large quadrangle, was considered too costly to execute. Edward Blore was commissioned to prepare a set of less ornate and costly elevations to be used with Baird's interiors. By 1849 when this compromise had been approved the Railway Company was in no state financially to honour any part of the Agreement and the scheme died.

PLATE 3
The Hunterian Museum behind the Old College was completed in 1804 to the designs of William Stark.

PLATE 4
The proposed new University at Woodlands. The second design by John Baird, 1846.

Gilmorehill

After the failure of the Woodlands scheme the University continued its occupation of the High Street property but dissatisfaction with the accommodation grew and from contemporary accounts it appears that the buildings had been allowed to fall into a certain degree of decay. In spite of a report by a Commission set up under the Universities (Scotland) Act that the College was unsuitable for teaching, no positive plans for an alternative were made until history repeated itself in 1863 with an offer of £100,000 from the City of Glasgow Union Railway Company who wished to acquire the High Street site as a goods yard.

An Act of Parliament was passed in 1863 to enable the College to sell the site and agreement reached with the Railway Company that they should have possession in five years. The lands of Gilmorehill extending to about 43 acres were considered along with other sites and purchased by the College for £65,000. The neighbouring lands of Donaldshill were purchased for a new infirmary. Additional money was raised by public subscription and a Treasury grant.

George Gilbert Scott, the famous London architect, was commissioned to draw up plans and work on the site began with the cutting of the first sod in 1866. When the New College Buildings Committee recommended Scott as the architect, they were probably influenced by the fact that he, more than any other, had experience in planning large buildings. In spite of their previous dissatisfaction with a local architect, the Committee sent Baird's plans to Scott. Doubtless these affected his design and his layout shows remarkable similarities. The first set of Baird's plans with its open quadrangles compares with the originally open west quadrangle of Scott's building; the second set is recalled in the two quadrangles and clock tower arrangement; and the third set in the location of the Library and Museum. Although the University was the largest building project in Britain since the Houses of Parliament, this was also the busiest period in Scott's career, with Government offices in Whitehall, St. Pancras Station and Hotel, and much other work in hand. It took him a year to produce the plans. (His only other

PLATE 5
The main staircase in the south wing by George Gilbert Scott (1870).

PLATE 6
The Humanity Class Room in the south-west corner of the Scott building still retains its original interior.

PLATE 7
The western block of Professors' Houses built to George Gilbert Scott's design in 1870.

Glasgow building is St. Mary's Cathedral on Great Western Road.) The choice of a London architect who was one of the leading exponents of the Gothic Revival style met with much criticism in a city which had preferred to build in a Victorian extension of Georgian classicism. Alexander (Greek) Thomson voiced the opinion that: "The less the Professors say about the artistic merits of the designs the better, and certainly local architects have nothing to fear from the invasion from the south." In his autobiography, Scott describes the style of the University as follows: "I have adopted a style which I may call my own invention.... It is simply a thirteenth or fourteenth century secular style with the addition of certain Scottish features."

For the sum of £190,000 – half what was being spent on St. Pancras Station – Scott provided the University with buildings of massive proportions measuring 540 feet by 300 feet, an unfinished tower and the foundations of a great hall which was to divide the east and west quadrangles (*cover*, Pls. 5 and 6). The west side of the west quadrangle was open until the 1920s, and to the west of this was built a square of tall houses as professorial residences (Pl. 7). The commonest criticism of the design is that the main façade has insufficient mass for its height, a defect inherent in the brief given to Scott. The omission of the originally intended southern terrace and stairway, by which he hoped to remedy this, has in fact aggravated it. In spite of these criticisms the front gives a grand and imposing appearance which cannot fail to please – particularly when seen in sharp perspective. The north front, gaining in scale from the full basement floor and dominated by the balconied apse of the Hunterian Museum entrance hall, provides an example of Scott at his best (Pl. 8). The pierced and patterned hollow girders and cast-iron pillars of the interior are an interesting example of iron construction in Gothic design.

The University took possession of its partially finished buildings in November 1870, having given over its High Street premises to the railway company on the 30th July. The teaching needs of the University were satisfied although the buildings were incomplete and as money for completion had run out, they might well have remained in this state for many years had it not been for a legacy from Charles Randolph, a local engineer and shipbuilder, and a gift from the Marquis of Bute in 1877 which enabled a great hall to be built and completed in 1882 (Pls. 9 and 10). The work was under-

PLATE 8
The North Front (1870) with the Hunterian Museum entrance hall on the right.

taken by Scott's son, John Oldrid Scott, and a building of soaring mediaeval romanticism with vaulted undercroft was created by the architect, probably influenced to a certain extent by the Marquis who was one of the architectural connoisseurs of the day. John Oldrid Scott finished the tower in 1887 with a graceful open-work stone spire (*cover*) in place of the St. Pancras type spire and clock envisaged by his father.

The Scott building – "a new and splendid edifice" – the museum on the north side of the east quadrangle, the library on the north side of the west quadrangle, teaching accommodation occupying the other wings and a great hall dividing the quadrangle, was, therefore, completed. The Lion and Unicorn staircase was removed from the Old College and erected in 1872 on the southwest corner, thus giving the Principal access from his house to the main building (Pl. 11). At the opposite end the Abbot's kitchen, an octagonal building used as a chemical laboratory, formed the south eastern extremity of the buildings.

Within a very short time of the completion of the main building, additional buildings began to appear. The generosity of Sir William Pearce, the engineer and shipbuilder, enabled part of the Old College façade to be erected as the Pearce Lodge at the northwest gate in 1887–8, thus preserving some of the architectural features of the earlier buildings. Need was felt for a students' union and in 1887 through the benefaction of John McIntyre, John J. Burnet, architect, erected a building with finely drawn detail, low proportions and a squat tower. It was, initially, the Men's Union; from 1931 it accommodated the Queen Margaret Union and is now the offices of the Students' Representative Council. It was extended by Burnet in 1893 and again in 1908. The Botany Building to the west of the Professors' houses, completed in 1901, and the Anatomy/Surgery and Engineering block (1902–03) to the east of the main building are by Burnet, who in both instances was influenced by "Scots Renaissance" style designs obtained by the University from John Oldrid Scott, making the result less pure in architectural style than his John McIntyre Building. The eastern block, which was extended by Burnet in 1908 and 1920 has some very fine features, although it is now somewhat screened by later developments.

The West Medical Building (Pl. 12) to the southwest of the main building, and Natural Philosophy (Pl. 13) were both the work of James Miller in 1907. They show rather elaborate early renaissance features giving an

PLATE 9
*The Bute Hall by John Oldrid Scott (1882)
seen from the east quadrangle.*

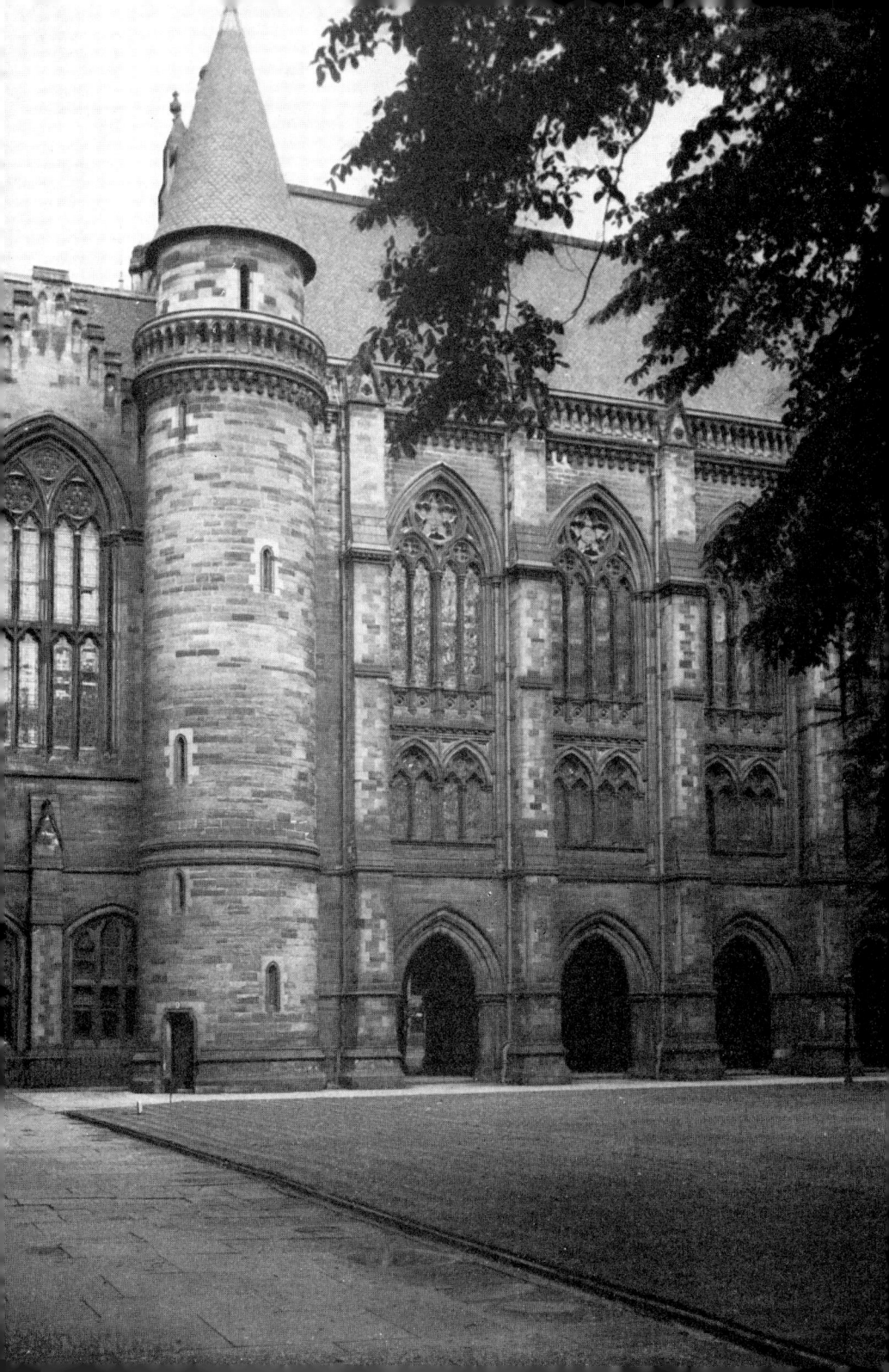

PLATE 10. *The east quadrangle seen through J. Oldrid Scott's undercroft of the Bute Hall.*

PLATE 12
One of the entrances to the West Medical Building, designed by James Miller in 1907.

PLATE 11. *The Lion and Unicorn Staircase was removed from the Old College and re-erected at the south west corner of the main building in 1872.*

attractive if somewhat fussy effect. Natural Philosophy was extended in 1954 and 1959 by Basil Spence and in 1966 by Basil Spence, Glover & Ferguson.

Proposals for a wing to close the west quadrangle had been under consideration in the years immediately prior to 1914 and Burnet had prepared drawings. With the advent of the First World War all expansion was halted and it was not until the 1920s that, in partnership with Norman A. Dick, Burnet designed the Memorial Chapel and connecting wings (1923–1929) (Pl. 14) understandably in a style more in the Scott tradition than his own, which manifested itself in the composition and detail of Zoology (1923) (Pl. 15) to the west of Natural Philosophy. The Students' Union (1931) in University Avenue shows marked Burnet influence and is the work of his former assistant, Alan McNaughton.

Modern architecture arrived in University extensions with the Chemistry Building which was started in 1936 but not completed until after the Second World War (1952). It is a fine example of inter-war design but its cramped site between Zoology and the Works Department makes an overall view impossible and the addition of the roof laboratory in 1963 and 1966 gives too much top hamper. The architects of Chemistry, T. Harold Hughes and D. S. R. Waugh, were responsible for the award-winning Reading Room (1939) (Pl. 16) on the north side of University Avenue.

In the post-war period the first building after the completion of Chemistry was the Boilerhouse (1952) to the east of the West Medical Building which was erected to the designs of Gillespie, Kidd & Coia. Keppie, Henderson & Partners were responsible for the James Watt Engineering Building completed in 1958 on the site occupied in part by the Abbot's kitchen; and for Biochemistry, to the east of the West Medical Buildings, which was completed in 1963. Other alterations and extensions to existing buildings were carried out but space was running short round the main building. New buildings, therefore, began to arise in Hillhead. The first of these was the Modern Languages Building, completed in 1959 by W. N. W. Ramsay, which replaced the Observatory in University Gardens. In 1960 the Physical Education Building rose in Oakfield Avenue to the design of Keppie, Henderson & Partners. The Institute of Virology (1961) situated beside Anderson's College of Medicine in Dumbarton Road is by Basil Spence & Partners and the Institute of Genetics (1966) in Church Street by Basil Spence, Glover & Ferguson.

PLATE 13

James Miller's Natural Philosophy Building (1907).

The Refectory by Frank Fielden & Associates (Pl. 16) behind the Reading Room, completed in 1966, swept away Charles Rennie Mackintosh's Southpark Avenue house, a replica of which is currently under reconstruction within the new University Art Gallery in Hillhead Street. The Adam Smith Building (1967) in Bute Gardens by David Harvey, Alex. Scott & Associates is over-shadowed by William Whitfield's Library (1968) whose towers dominate the area as dramatically as that of the Scott building and strikingly balance it. The Queen Margaret Union (1968) by Walter Underwood & Partners, and the Mathematics Building (1969) (Pl. 17) by J. C. Gleave & Partners occupy sites in University Gardens. The Boyd Orr Basic Science Building (1972) (Pl. 17) by Dorward, Matheson, Gleave & Partners is situated in what was formerly Ashton Road, and the Rankine Building (1969) in Oakfield Avenue by Keppie, Henderson & Partners, complete the list of major works in the Hillhead area. The Art Gallery by William Whitfield and the Geology Building in Lilybank Gardens by Dorward, Matheson, Gleave & Partners are at the time of writing unfinished.

In addition to the new buildings in the Hillhead area, the University has acquired a large amount of terraced property. The finest of these terraces is University Gardens which has in recent years been cleaned and restored. The graceful curve of numbers 1–10 (Pl. 18) is by John J. Burnet (*c*. 1896) while numbers 12 and 14 are by Salmon, Son & Gillespie (*c*. 1901) but are probably largely the work of J. Gaff Gillespie. They are excellent examples of the work of less well-known exponents of art nouveau. The work of Alexander (Greek) Thomson is found at numbers 27–53 Oakfield Avenue (*c*. 1865) and in the extension to Lilybank House (*c*. 1850) which has happily found a safe haven amidst its towering concrete neighbours. Gilmorehill Church, converted for examinations and known as Gilmorehill Hall (1878), is by James Sellars and still sadly awaits its planned spire! Sellars was also responsible for Anderson's College Medical School (1888) in Dumbarton Road. Southpark House (1850 – architect unknown) was converted in 1967 for the University television studios.

The Garscube complex of buildings, which were built between 1957 and 1970 mainly to accommodate the Veterinary Hospital and School, are the work of Gillespie, Kidd & Coia; W. N. W. Ramsay; Building Design Partnership; Wylie, Shanks & Partners; and Boswell, Mitchell & Johnson.

PLATE 14
The University Chapel and West Wing, built 1923–29 to designs by John J. Burnet, seen from Oldrid Scott's undercroft.

The Hydrodynamics Laboratory and the Observatory in Acre Road are by Keppie, Henderson & Partners in 1966 and 1967 respectively. The Zoology Field Station, Loch Lomond (1964) by Thomson, McCrea & Sanders and the Veterinary Field Station, Cochno (1967) by Lothian Barclay, Jarvis & Boys, together with student and staff recreational centres, halls of residence, and various other minor structures old and new, complete the picture of the University's buildings.

Major reconstruction has taken place over the years of the original building, rendering its interiors in some cases almost unrecognisable from Scott's concept. The pattern of a continuing building programme will no doubt accompany the University into the twenty-first century.

PLATE 15. *The Zoology Building (1923) by John J. Burnet.*

PLATE 16
The award-winning Reading Room, built 1938/9 to designs by T. Harold Hughes and D. S. R. Waugh, with the Refectory by Frank Fielden and Associates in the background, seen from the University Tower.

List of University Buildings

HIGH STREET
1470–1632	Original tenements
1632–1870	The Old College Buildings
1774–1870	Library: William Adam
1804–1870	Hunterian Museum: William Stark
1811–1870	Hamilton Buildings: Peter Nicholson

GILMOREHILL and HILLHEAD
1870	Main Buildings and Professors' Houses: George Gilbert Scott
1872	Lion and Unicorn Staircase
1882	Bute and Randolph Halls: John Oldrid Scott
1887	Spire: John Oldrid Scott
1887/8	Pearce Lodge
1887	John McIntyre Building ⎫
1893	John McIntyre Building extended ⎬ John J. Burnet
1908	John McIntyre Building extended ⎭
1901	Botany: John Burnet
1902/3	Anatomy/Surgery and Engineering ⎫
1908	Anatomy/Surgery and Engineering extended ⎬ John J. Burnet
1920	Engineering extended ⎭
1907	West Medical Building: James Miller
1907	Natural Philosophy: James Miller
1954	Extension I Basil Spence
1959	Extension II Basil Spence & Partners
1966	Extension III Basil Spence, Glover & Ferguson
1923	Zoology: John Burnet
1925	William and George Hunter Memorial: John J. Burnet
1923–29	West Wing and Chapel: John (J.) Burnet, Son & Dick
1931	Students' Union (Men): Alan McNaughton
1965	Students' Union (Men) extension: Keppie, Henderson & Partners
1937	Stevenson Laboratory: T. Harold Hughes and D. S. R. Waugh
1939	Reading Room: T. Harold Hughes and D. S. R. Waugh
1936 ⎫ 1952 ⎭	Chemistry Building: T. Harold Hughes and D. S. R. Waugh
1963 ⎫ 1966 ⎭	Chemistry Building Roof Laboratories: Alexander Wright & Kay
1952	The Boilerhouse: Gillespie, Kidd & Coia

PLATE 17

The Boyd Orr Building, built for Basic Science teaching, completed in 1972 to designs by Dorward, Matheson, Gleave and Partners. Mathematics (1969), by J. C. Gleave and Partners is on the right.

1958	Engineering South: Keppie, Henderson & Partners
1959	Modern Languages: W. N. W. Ramsay
1960	Physical Education: Keppie, Henderson & Partners
1961	Institute of Virology: Basil Spence & Partners
1963	Biochemistry Building: Keppie, Henderson & Partners
1966	Refectory: Frank Fielden & Associates
1966	Institute of Genetics: Basil Spence, Glover & Ferguson
1967	Adam Smith Building: David Harvey, Alex. Scott & Associates
1968	Queen Margaret Union: Walter Underwood & Partners
1968	Library I: William Whitfield
1969	Mathematics Building ⎫ J. C. Gleave & Partners
1969	New Senate Room ⎭
1969	Rankine Building: Keppie, Henderson & Partners
1972	Boyd Orr Building: Dorward, Matheson, Gleave & Partners
Incomplete	Art Gallery: William Whitfield
,,	Geology Building: Dorward, Matheson, Gleave & Partners

GARSCUBE

1957	Veterinary Hospital Garscube Main Building: Gillespie, Kidd & Coia
1960	Wellcome Surgical Laboratory and Extension I ⎫ W. N. W. Ramsay
1962	Large Animal Units ⎭
1964	Wellcome Parasitology
1964	Equine Unit and Foal House
1968	Large Animal Unit
1969	Veterinary School I ⎫ Building Design
1969	Veterinary Surgery and Reproduction Units ⎪ Partnership
1969	Wellcome Surgical Extension II
1969	Garscube Refectory
1970	Veterinary School II ⎭
1960	Hydrodynamics Laboratory: Keppie, Henderson & Partners
1966	Botany Research Laboratory: Wylie, Shanks & Partners
1967	Observatory: Keppie, Henderson & Partners
1970	Alexander Stone Building: Boswell, Mitchell & Johnston
Incomplete	Royal Beatson Hospital: Boswell, Mitchell & Johnston

MISCELLANEOUS

c.1850	Southpark House
1967	Alterations for Television Studio: Thomas, McCrea & Sanders
c.1850	Lilybank House
c.1856	Extension: Alexander Thomson
1865	27–53 Oakfield Avenue: Alexander Thomson
1878	Gilmorehill Church: James Sellars
1963	Alterations: Keppie, Henderson & Partners

PLATE 18
University Gardens from University Avenue. The part seen here was designed by John J. Burnet and completed c.1896.

1888	Anderson's College: James Sellars
	Alterations: John Keppie, Henderson & J. L. Gleave
1896	University Gardens 1–10: J. J. Burnet
1901	University Gardens 12 and 14: Salmon, Son & Gillespie
1923	Westerlands: James M. Honeyman
1936	Garscadden: T. Harold Hughes and D. S. R. Waugh
1958	Extension: Alexander Wright & Kay
1960	Staff Recreation Garscube: W. J. Fairweather
1967	Extension: W. N. W. Ramsay
1966	Squash Courts Garscube: D. C. Bailey
1964	Zoology Field Station, Loch Lomond: Thomas McCrea & Sanders
1964	Queen Margaret Hall I ⎫ W. N. W. Ramsay
1967	Queen Margaret Hall II ⎭
1964	Wolfson Hall I ⎫ Building Design Parternership
1968	Wolfson Hall II ⎭
1965	Dalrymple Hall: W. N. W. Ramsay
1967	Maclay Hall I ⎫ W. N. W. Ramsay
1969	Maclay Hall II ⎭
1967	Veterinary Field Station, Cochno: Lothian Barclay, Jarvis & Boys